A Mark Dahle Portfolio

Amanda Gets A Watermelon

(#2 in the series Amanda Wanted A Miracle)

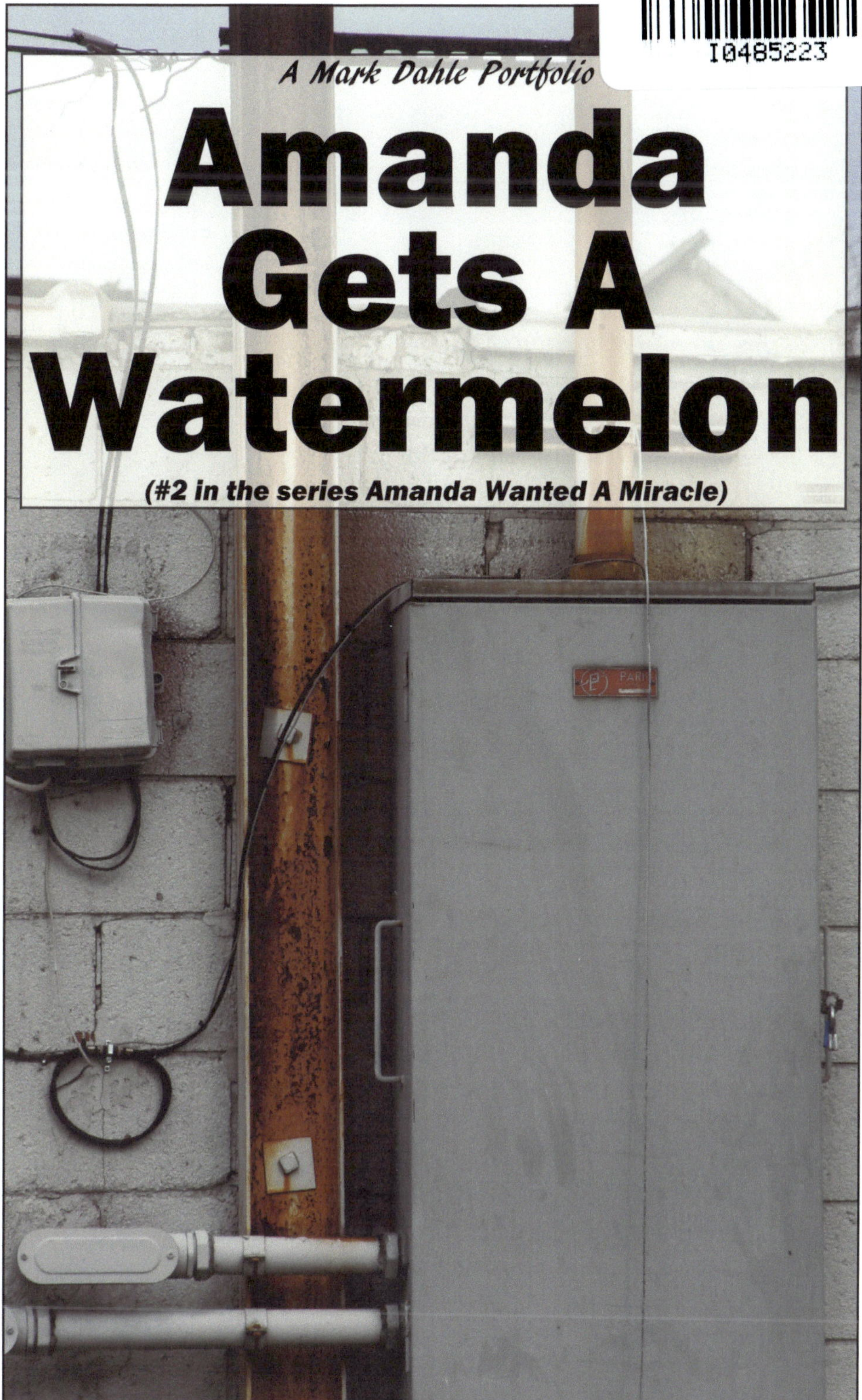

This is the second story in the series "Amanda Wanted A Miracle." The books in this series:
> 1. Amanda Gets A Pumpkin
> 2. Amanda Gets A Watermelon
> 3. Amanda Gets A Surprise
> 4. Amanda Gets A Neighbor
> 5. Amanda Gets A Miracle

~ ~ ~

Mark Dahle Portfolios can be read in a few minutes and enjoyed for a lifetime.

Unlike many picture books, the text in this book is not related to the art. This might seem weird at first. One thing that makes it better is to order more portfolios until you get used to it. Fortunately, space is provided on the pages for you to draw your own pictures of watermelons if you like.

This portfolio includes a photo of a beautiful 36 x 24 inch painting (at the right), twenty-four great photos from Detroit, Michigan, and a story about Amanda, who wanted a miracle but got a watermelon instead.

Photographs in this book are available in limited editions. See http://www.MarkDahle.com for more information and for previews of upcoming portfolios.

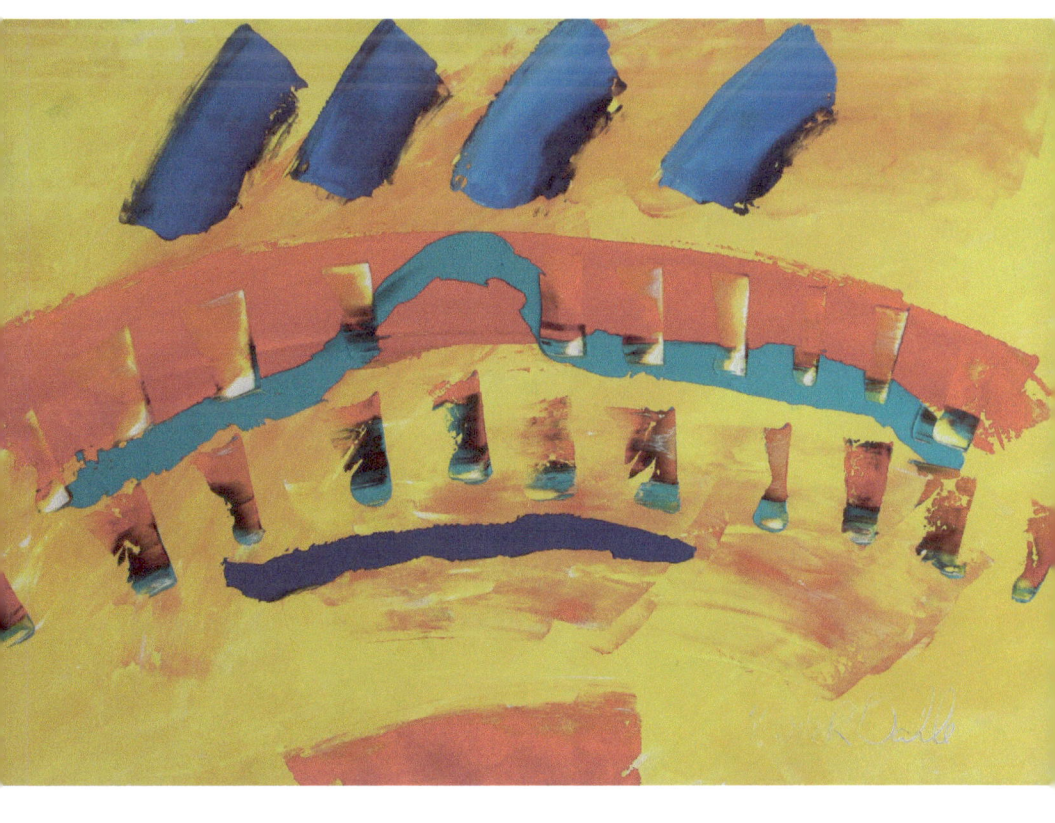

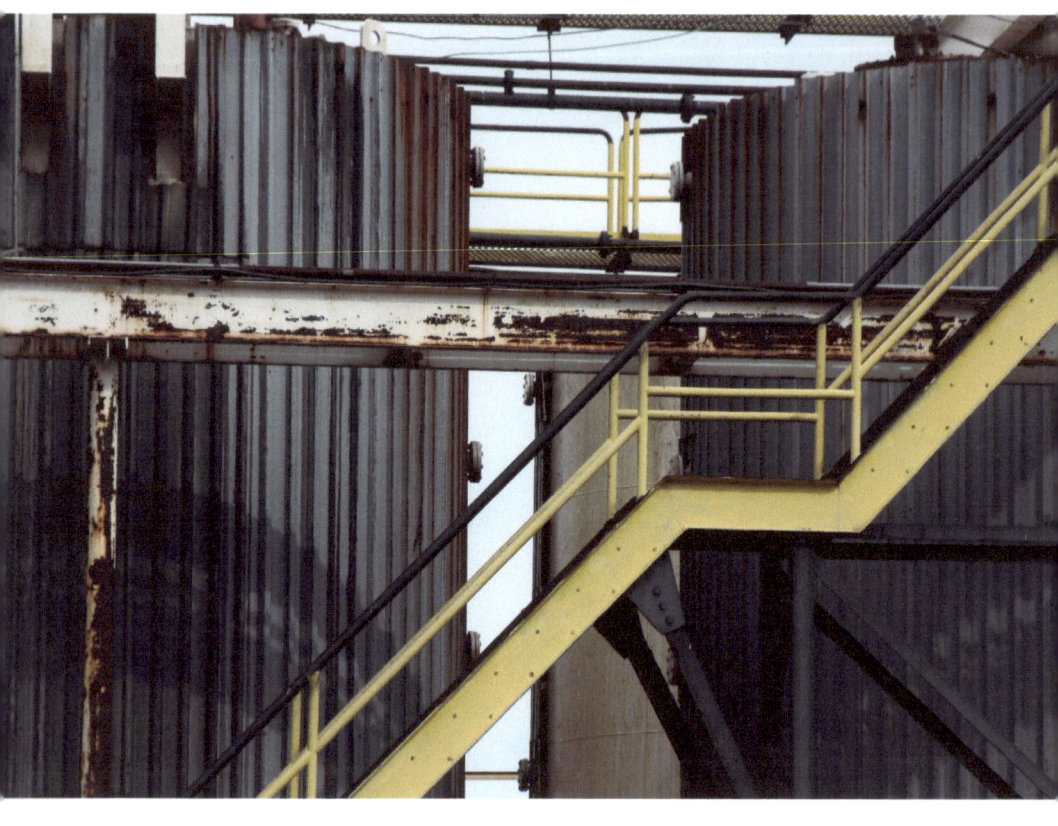

Amanda sat beside her grandmother at the breakfast table. "I saw you last night," she said.

Her grandmother didn't flinch.

"Yes, dear," she said. "We sat at the table and had milk and cookies."

"No," said Amanda. "After that. After I went to bed."

Her grandmother didn't say anything. She had been pulling pumpkins out of the air and putting them back, just for practice.

"I got thirsty," said Amanda. "I got up to get some water. I was about to step into the kitchen when I saw you pull a pumpkin out of the air."

"You were probably dreaming, dear."

Amanda stamped her foot. "I was *not* dreaming. You did it five or six times."

Amanda's grandmother sighed. Actually, she had probably done it five or six *hundred* times that night. She had been a little bored with babysitting after Amanda had gone to bed and she had needed practice with her pumpkins.

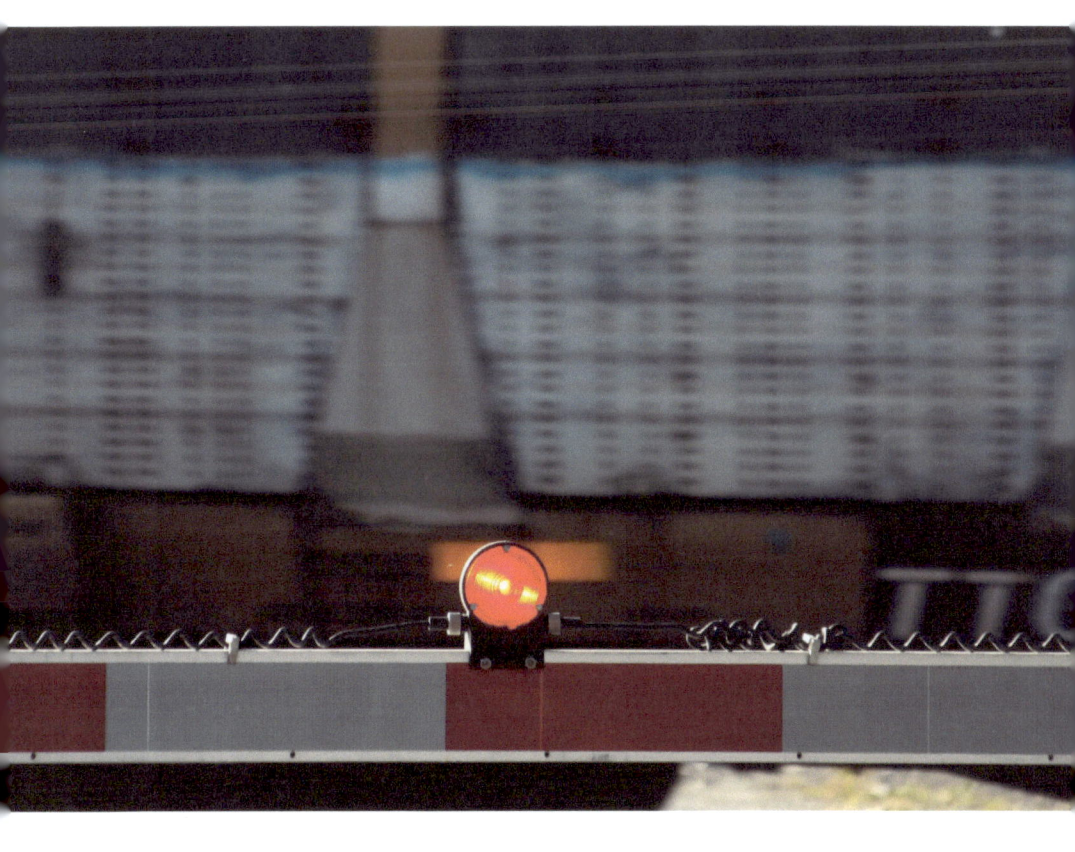

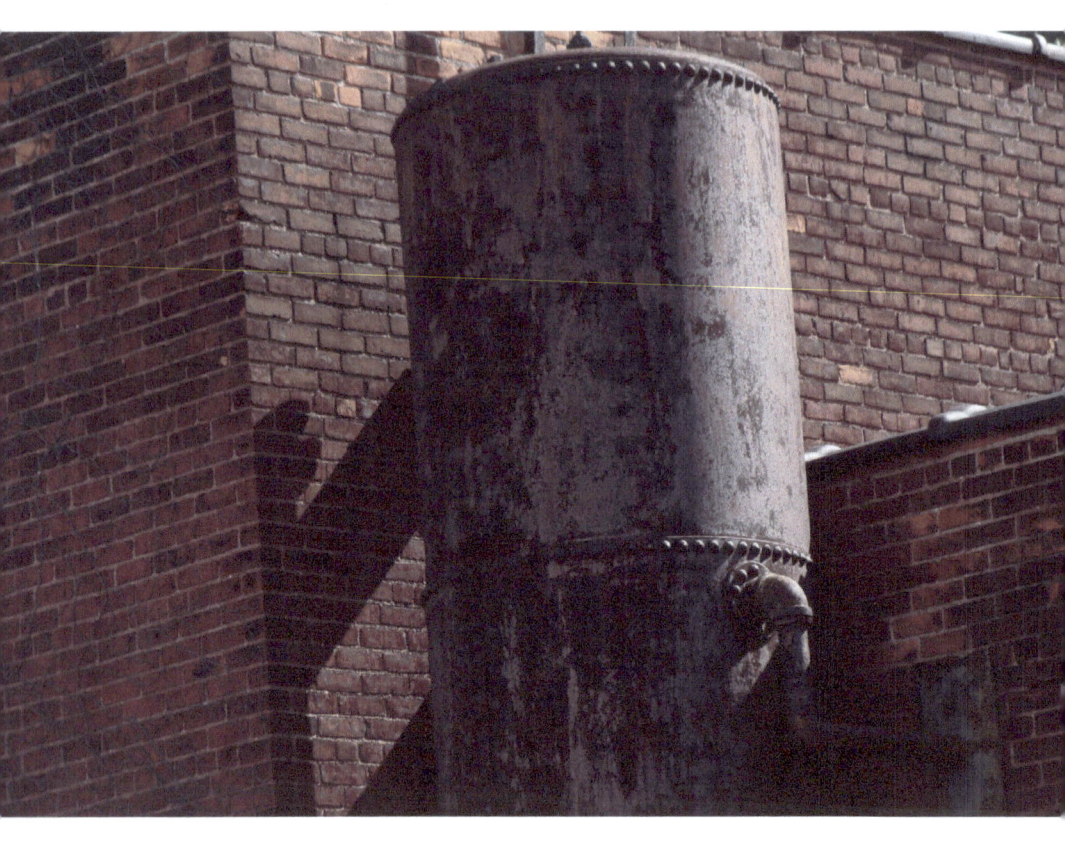

"Suppose that's true, dear," she said. "Then what?"

Amanda didn't know.

But she did soon enough. "I want to learn how to pull pumpkins out of the air!" she said.

"Well, dear," said her grandmother, "I can teach you that. But learning how to do it takes a lot of hard work. Usually. Are you sure you want to learn how to do pumpkins?"

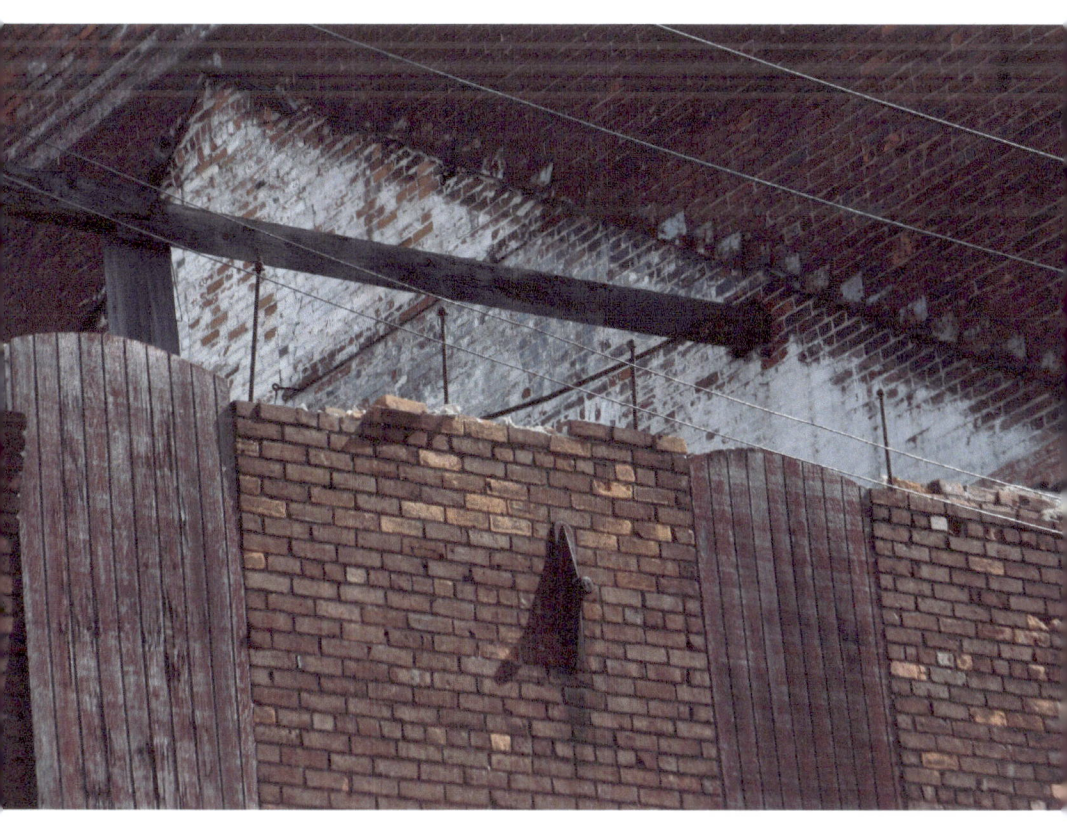

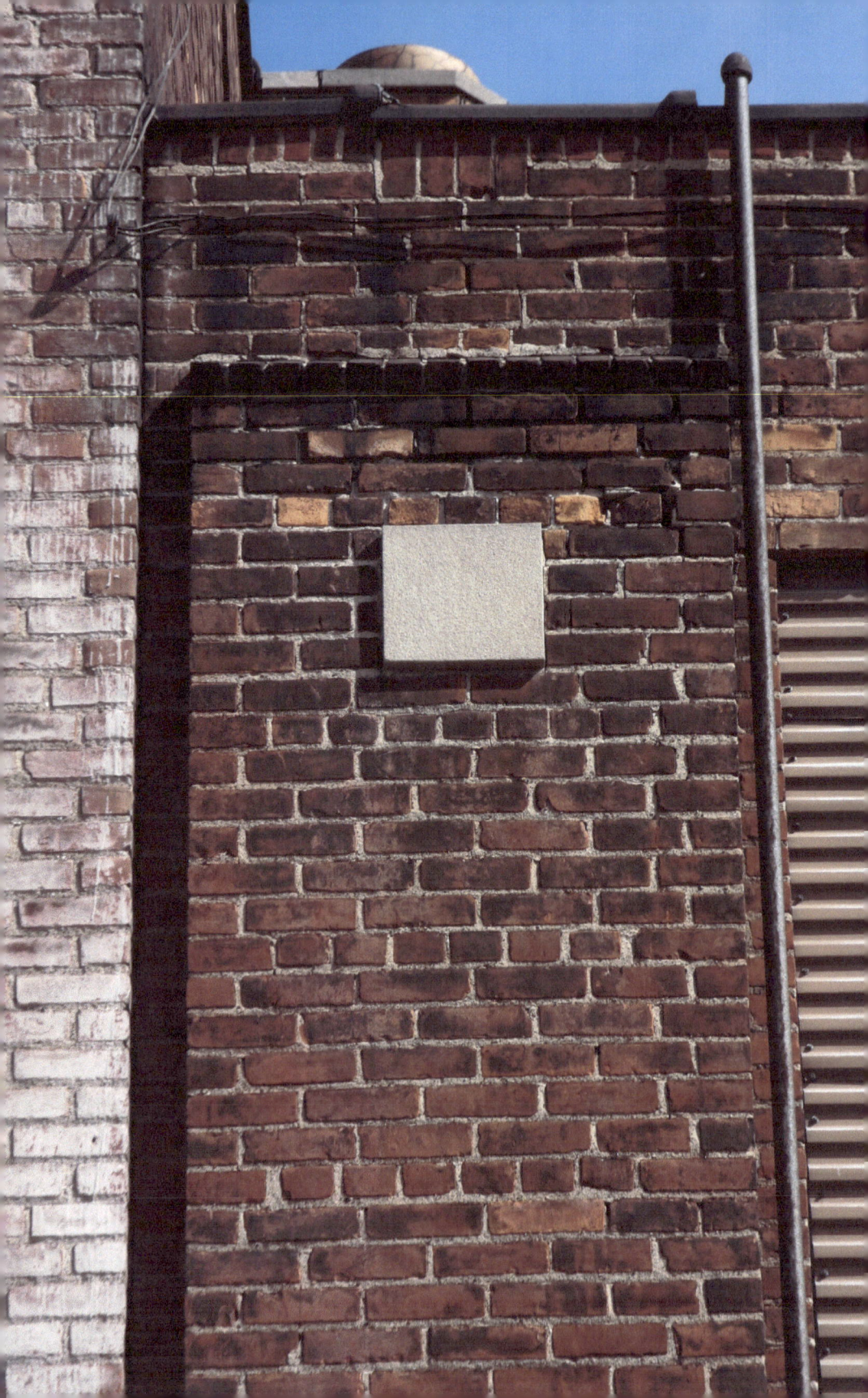

Amanda didn't have to think for long. She already had a stack of pumpkins on the porch. She didn't need more pumpkins. She wanted a miracle. She told her grandmother. Again.

"Oh," said her grandmother. "To get *that* kind of miracle, you'll have to call your grandfather."

Amanda froze. She wondered why her grandmother hadn't told her this before. Amanda had spent the whole summer growing pumpkins. Was all that time wasted? Plus, she was a little afraid of her grandfather. He never sat down for a nice talk with cookies and milk. He was frightfully busy most of the time. Or at least he thought he was.

"Is there anybody else I could talk to?"

"No, dear. He's the best if you want that kind of miracle."

Amanda had some breakfast while she tried to get up her courage. Then she called her grandfather.

"Hi, Amanda," he answered. "How can I help you?"

"I want to learn how to do a miracle."

"Perhaps you should talk to your grandmother. She's very good with pumpkins."

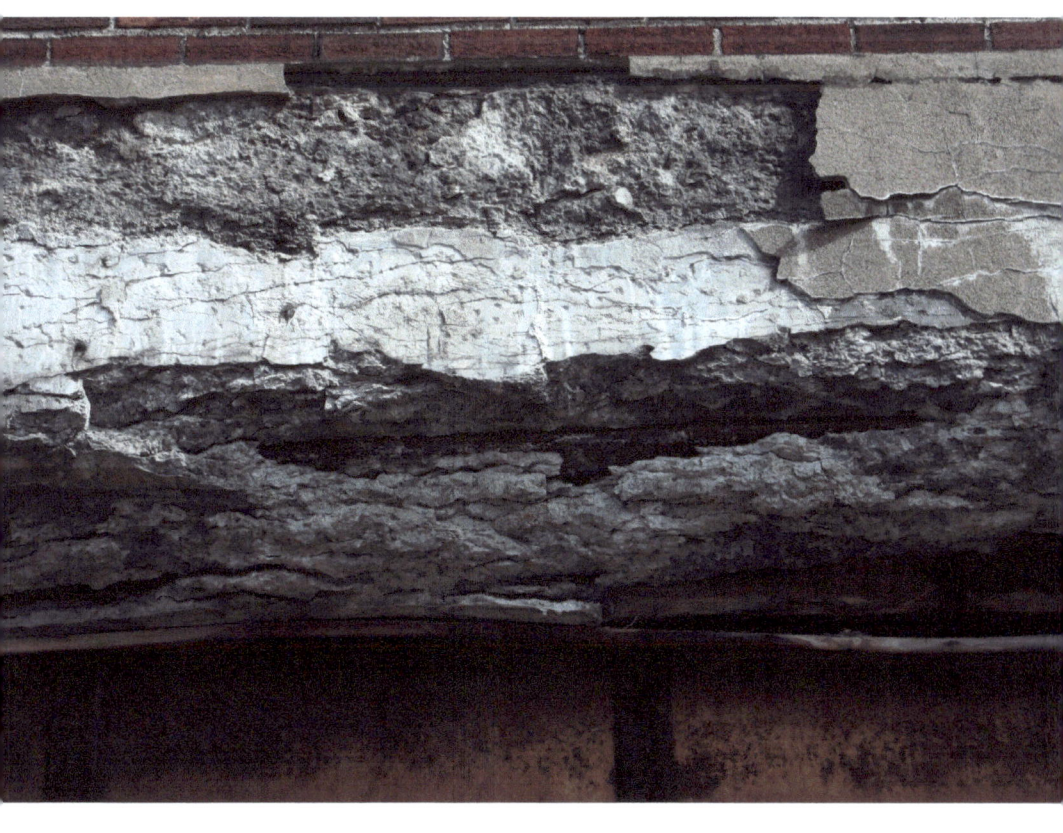

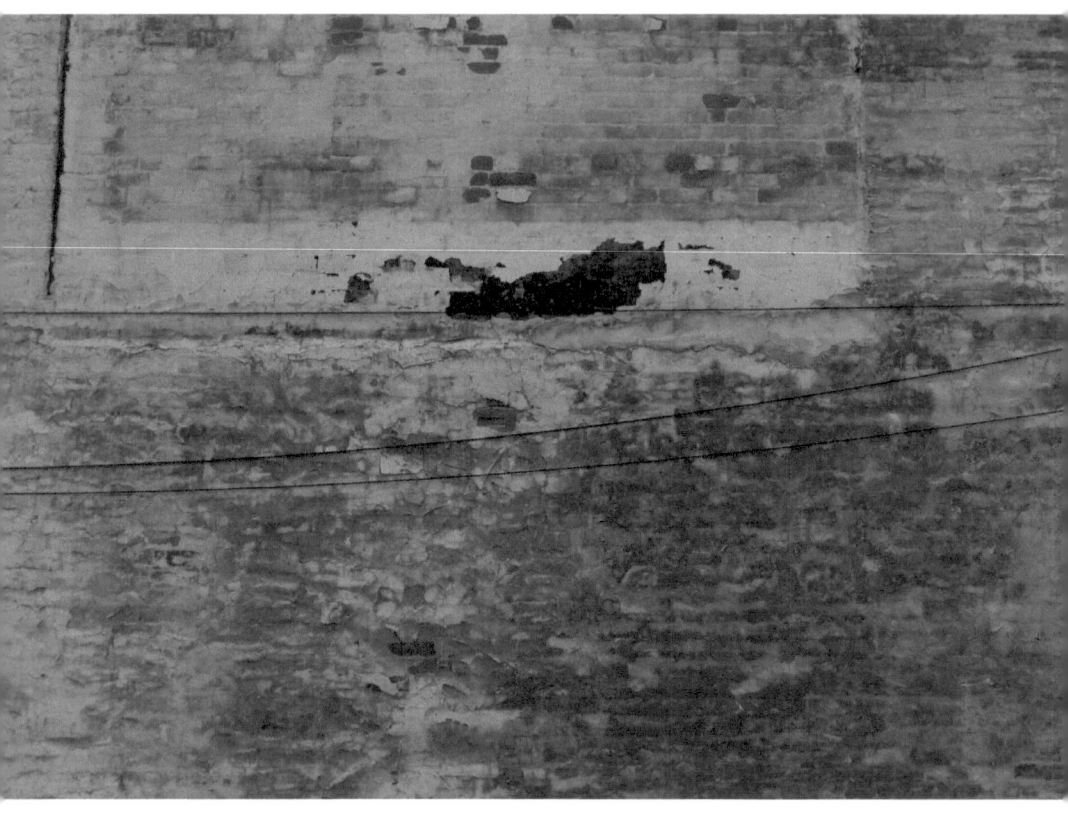

"No," Amanda said. She told her grandfather about the miracle she wanted.

"Oh," he said. "I see. Well, yes, I suppose a pumpkin wouldn't do for that. Tuesday. 6 p.m. My place. Don't be late." He hung up.

"Well, dear?" said her grandmother.

"He said I had to be at his house on Tuesday at 6. How will I do *that*?"

They didn't know.

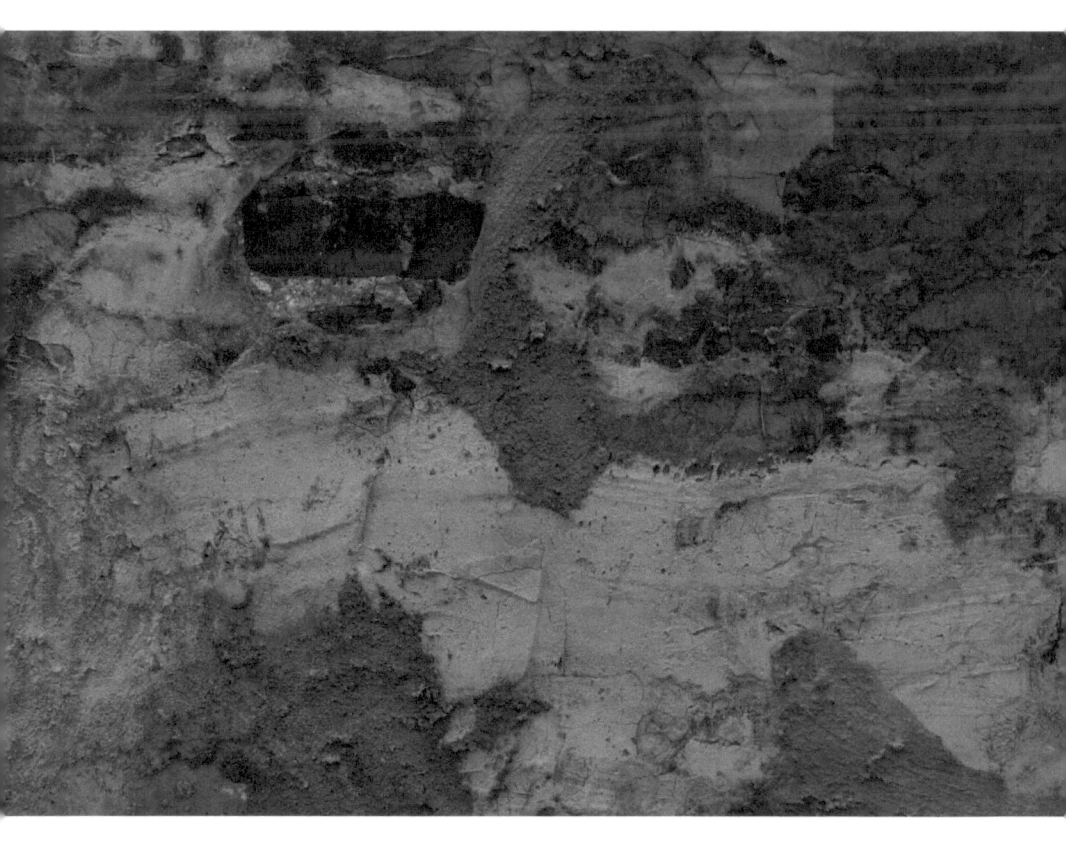

The phone rang.

"Hello?" said Amanda.

"I forgot to tell you. Take the Number Six bus from your house promptly at 5:45. Tell the driver you want Elmsworth Drive. He'll stop right at my house. Usually." Then he hung up. It had been her grandfather.

When Amanda told her grandmother the details, her grandmother's eyes narrowed. "That old bird never takes the bus and he doesn't know what he's talking about," she sputtered. "The Number Six is the least reliable bus in the fleet."

After a pause, she said "I'll go with you. . ." She had been going to say, "to keep you safe" but at the last minute she switched to saying "just in case."

Just in case what? Amanda didn't know. But in the meantime, she had lots of work to do before Tuesday. She was trying to sell the stack of pumpkins she had grown over the summer to raise money for her miracle.

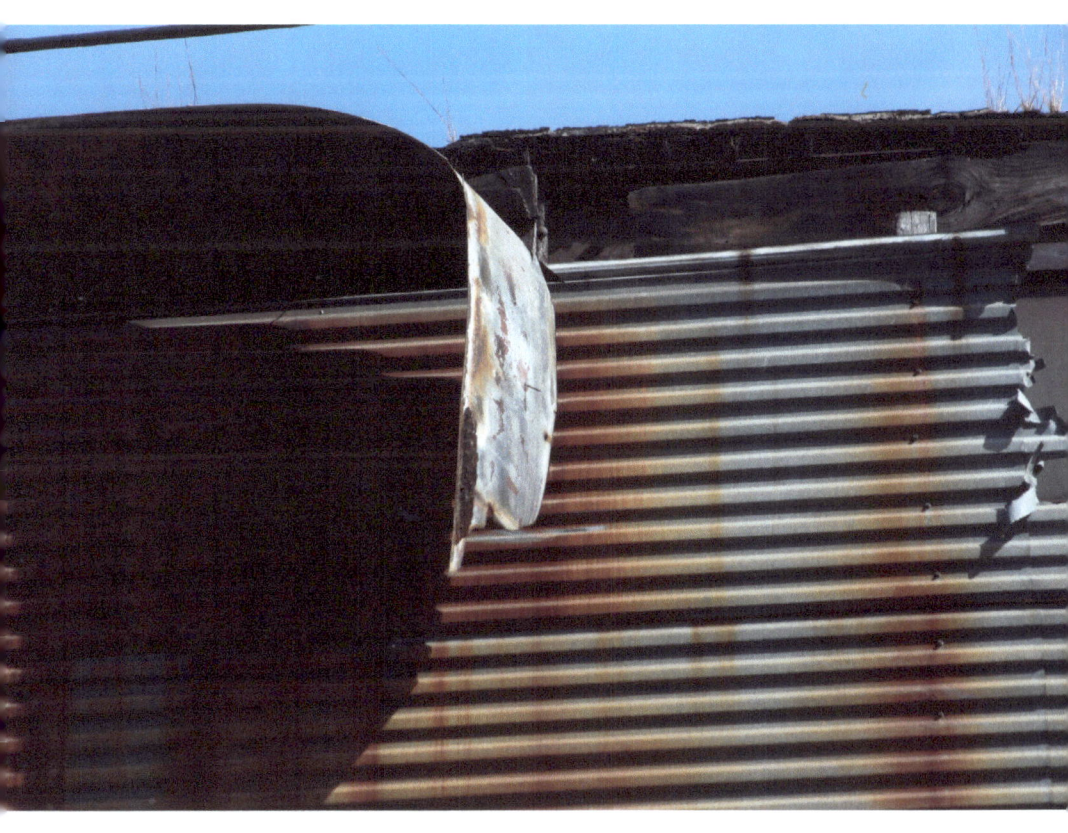

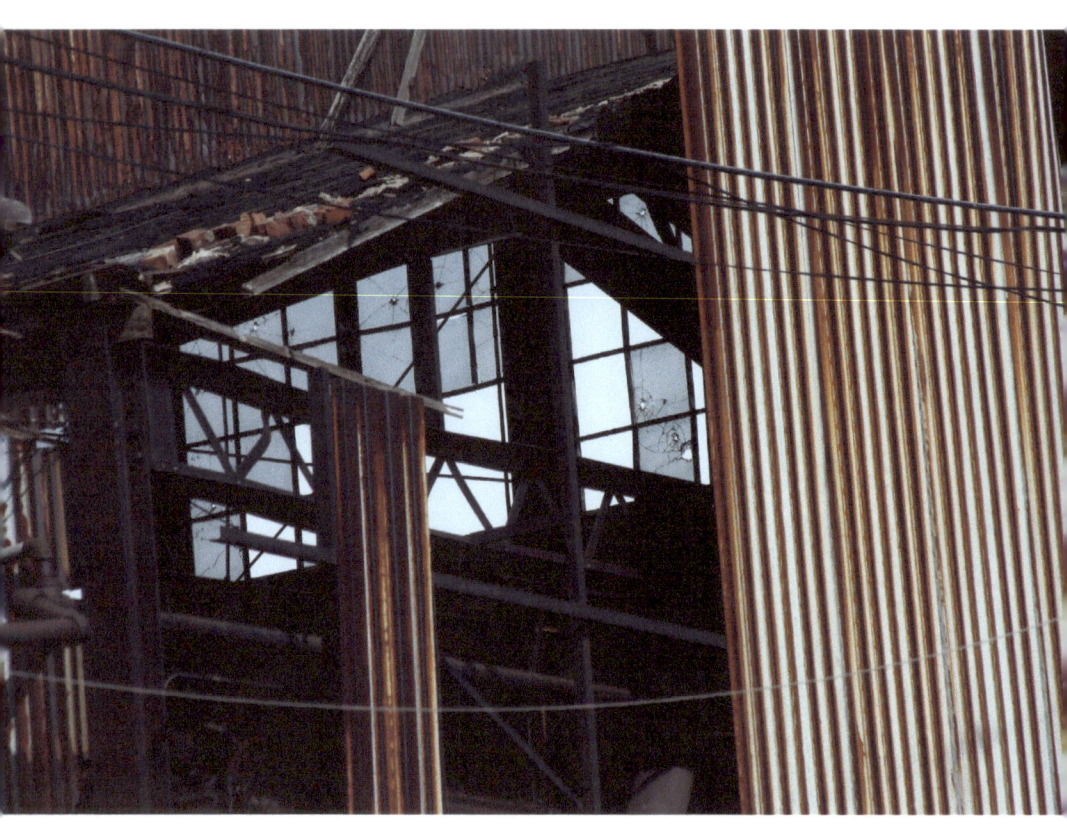

When Tuesday came, Amanda was standing outside her house at 5:45 with her grandmother. They had arrived at the corner ten minutes early, just in case.

But the bus didn't come early. Or at 5:45. It wasn't there at 5:46. Or at 5:47. Or 5:48. Or 5:49.

Amanda was becoming afraid that she'd be late for her grandfather's when she heard a fierce rattling and an old red bus rounded the corner, stopping right in front of her. The front bumper was tied to the bus with a string. Amanda looked at the bumper, then shrugged and boarded the bus. Her grandmother gave the driver two of Amanda's pumpkins for their fares.

Amanda had wanted to use two of the pumpkins her grandmother pulled from the air, but she said Amanda's would be better. "Home grown, you know." Amanda didn't know, but she kept her mouth shut.

They had barely taken their seats when a bright blue flash lit up the interior of the bus. "Elmsworth Drive," the driver said, opening the door again. "Better hurry. The old man doesn't like people to be late."

Looking out, Amanda found to her surprise that they were already at her grandfather's. But she hesitated when she saw her grandmother wasn't getting out with her.

"You go ahead, dear," her grandmother said. "I'll wait here with the driver and keep him company. That way the bus will be here when you want to go home."

"You're not coming with me?"

"It'll be better this way. Maybe next time." She kissed Amanda on the forehead.

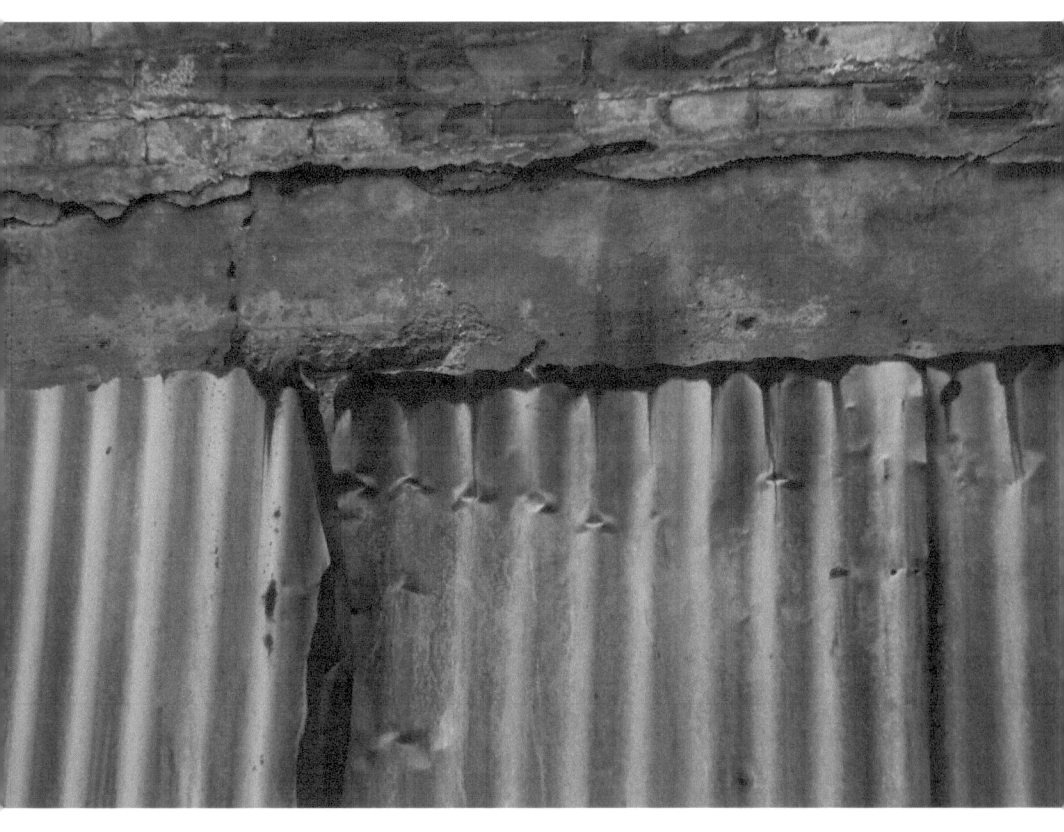

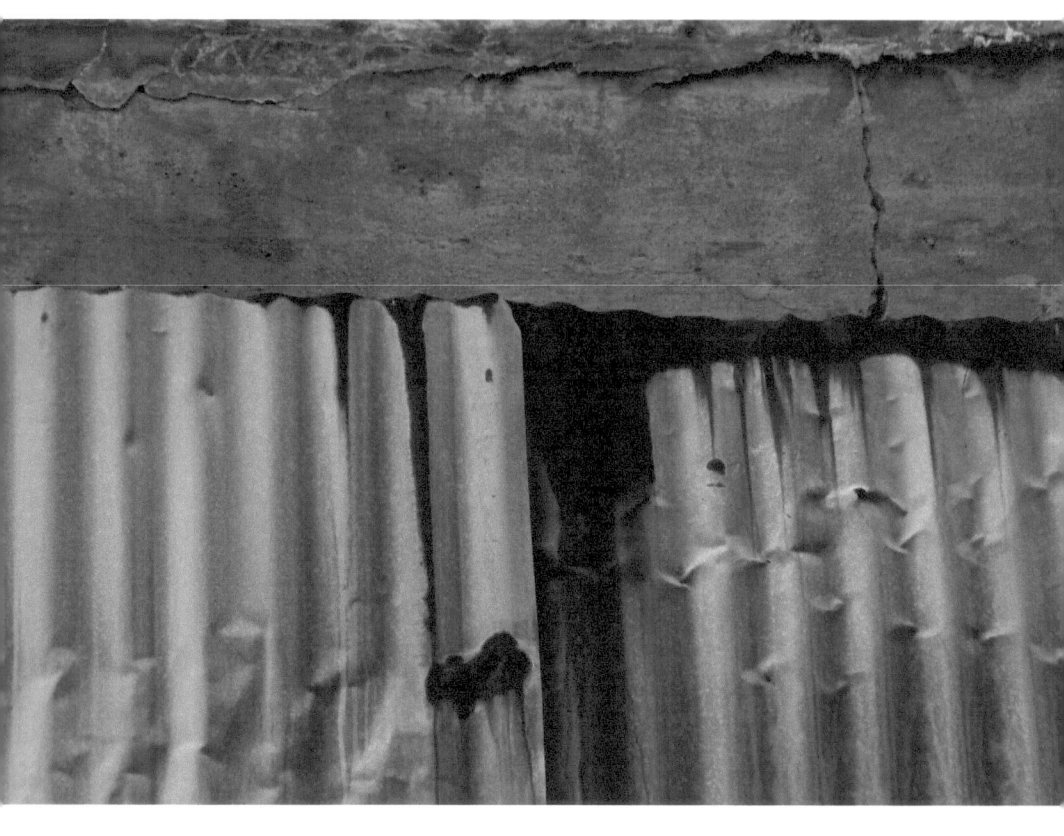

Amanda wasn't sure she was brave enough to see her grandfather by herself, but at 5:59 she rang the doorbell of his immense house.

He arrived, pocket watch in hand, at exactly six.

"Amanda!" he said. "So good to see you! It's been too long. But I only have five minutes. Close your eyes and hold out your hands."

Amanda did as commanded and soon found she was holding something heavier than a pumpkin. More smooth than one, too. She peeked with one eye. Just what she thought. A watermelon.

She had the feeling she had been through this before. She opened her eyes.

"Oh!" she said. "A watermelon. Very nice."

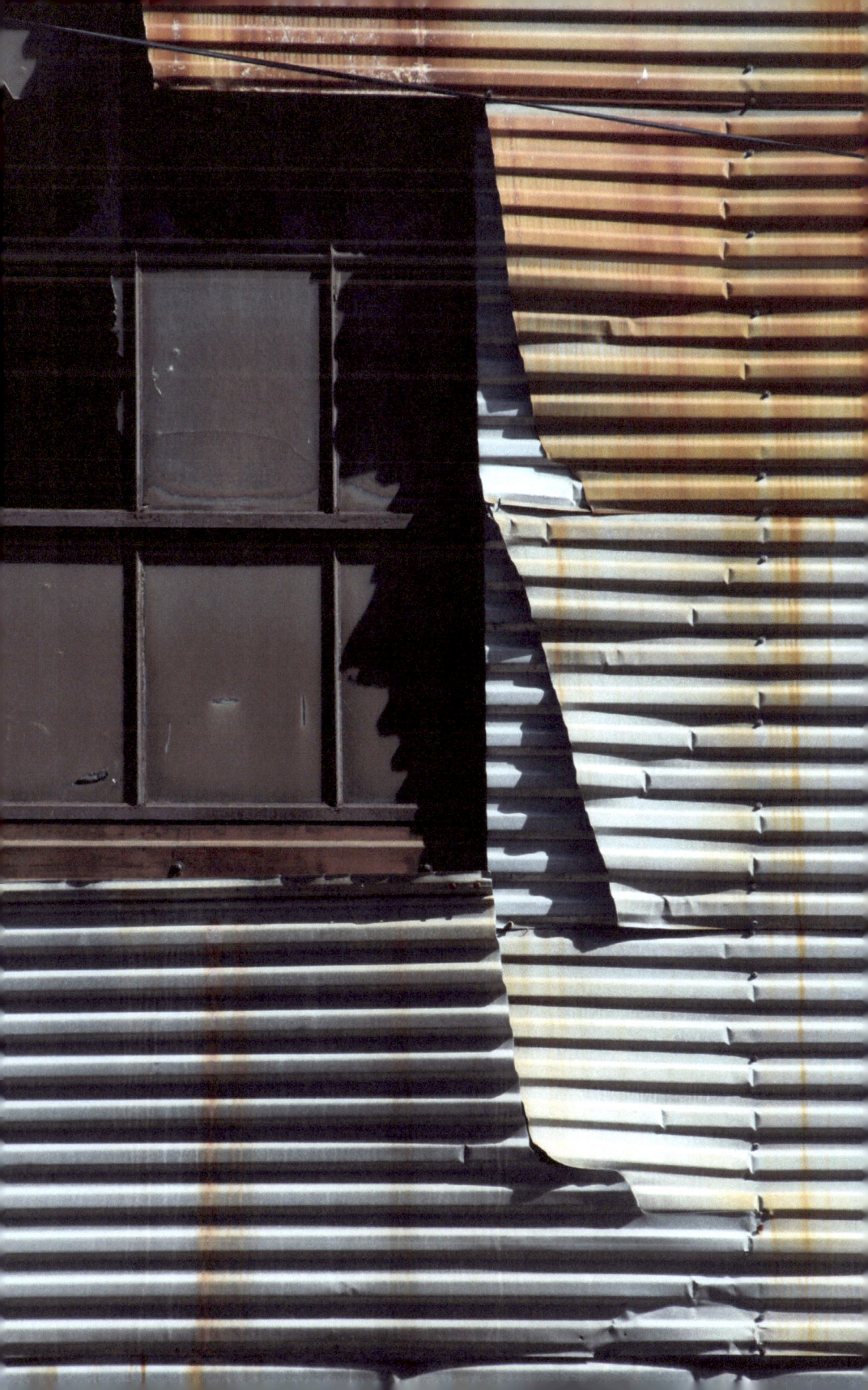

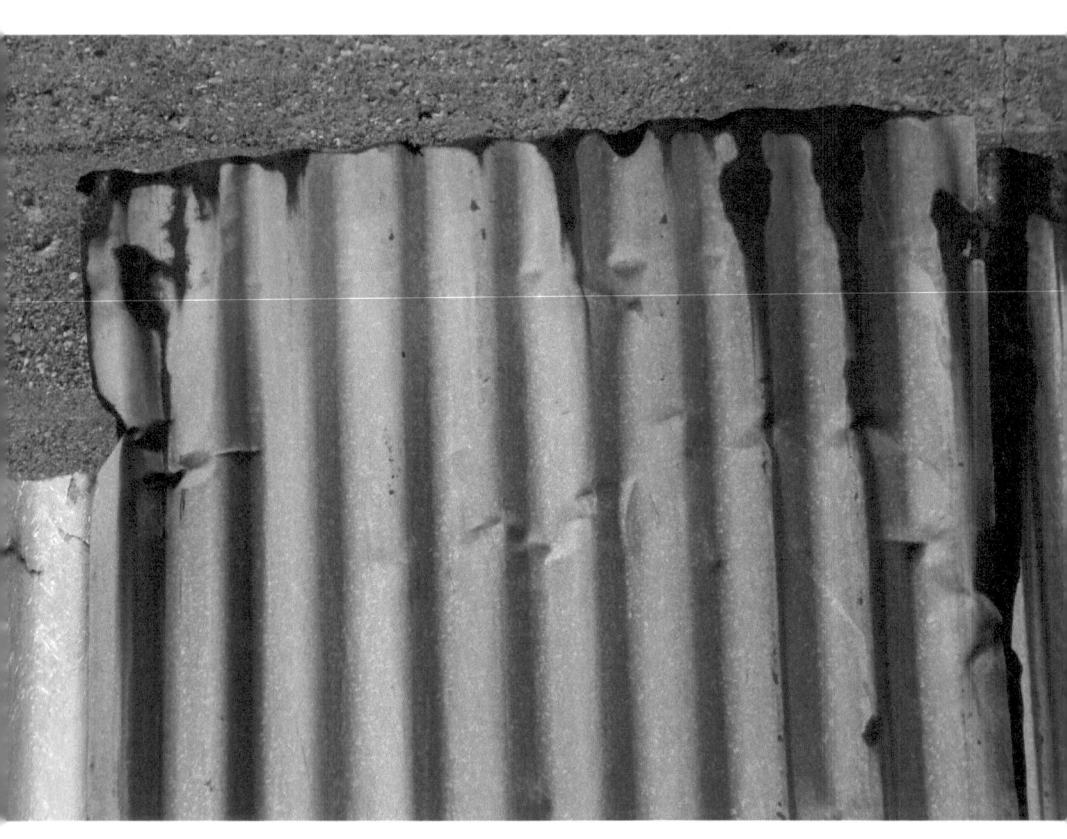

"We're in a rush," said her grandfather, "so let's skip the pleasantries. It's green, round, very nice shape, but not what you wanted. You want a miracle instead. Right?"

Amanda was startled at how well he knew her. She nodded that he was correct.

"Okay," he said. "Perhaps we'll have to start again. Put the watermelon on the porch." Amanda obeyed. "Now close your eyes and stretch out your hands."

Amanda did, and just as she expected, something light dropped into them. She didn't have to look. Three seeds. Watermelon seeds, no doubt.

"Grandpa," she said, opening her eyes, "I've done this before. With pumpkins."

He stood up taller than before and snorted. "Pumpkins! You dare to compare my beautiful watermelon with *pumpkins?*" He looked hurt. "Anyway, it doesn't matter," he said. "You missed the point. But I'm pretty sure you can do it with your eyes open, too. Put the seeds in your pocket – you'll need them later."

Amanda obeyed. Her five minutes were almost up and she still didn't have her miracle.

"Okay," he said, "stretch out your hands. And this time keep your eyes open."

Amanda did so, and when she stretched out her hands, a pumpkin appeared in them. A fairly small pumpkin, more green than orange, but a pumpkin, never-the-less. Her grandfather hadn't put it there. She had just stretched out her hands and there it was.

Amanda blinked with surprise. She didn't know how it had happened. But she didn't have much time to ponder what she had done.

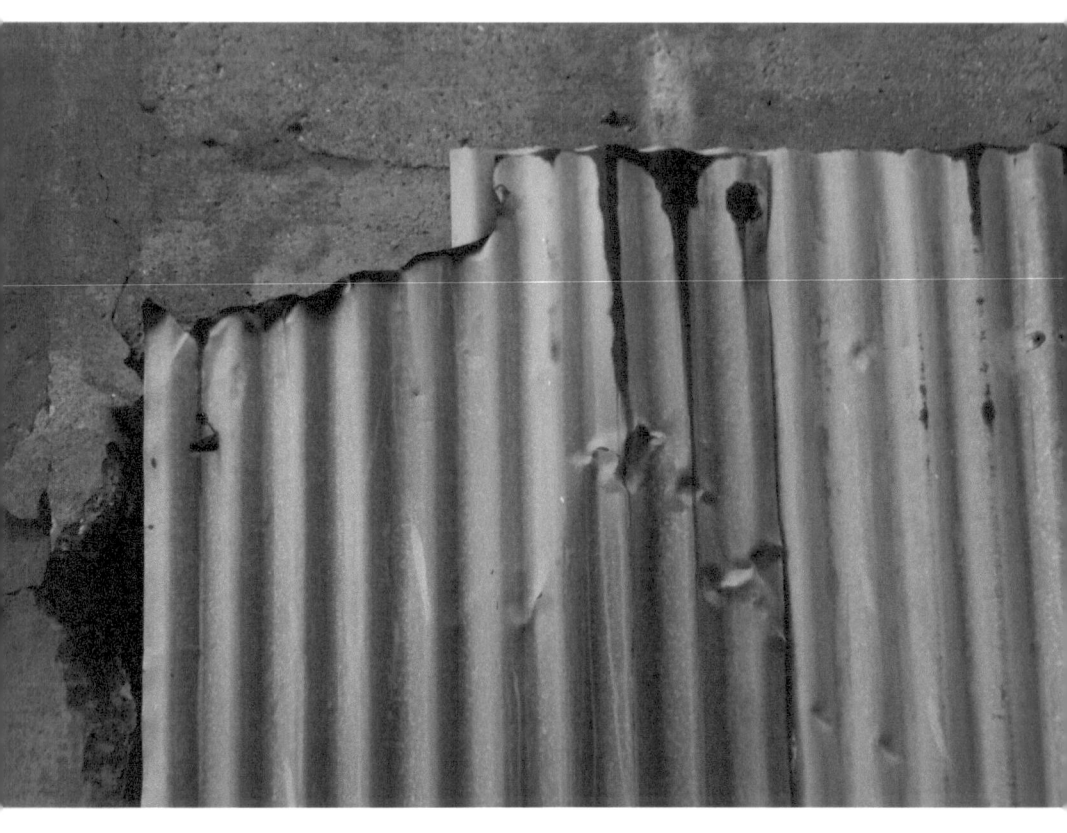

Her grandfather snorted again. "A pumpkin! Hah! I should have guessed. How typical. Too much time with your grandmother, no doubt. But our time's up. Go home and plant the seeds and take care of them. Maybe you'll get a nice round watermelon before too long. Or something even better. Who knows. Good to see you, Amanda."

He looked at his watch, decided he had enough time, and bent down and kissed her on the forehead. Then he went back inside the house and closed the door. They had been standing on the porch the whole time.

Amanda didn't think her grandfather knew very much about being polite to company (or relatives). But she thought he might know something about miracles. She wasn't sure. It was a little confusing. She really didn't want watermelons any more than she wanted pumpkins.

Amanda put her small, green pumpkin on the porch beside the watermelon. She stretched out her hands again and another pumpkin appeared in them, this one slightly bigger and more orange. But this one was made of porcelain.

Amanda wasn't sure how she was getting the pumpkins, but she collected the watermelon and her two pumpkins and headed down the steps before she had too much to carry.

As she walked, Amanda thought about the seeds in her pocket. She had spent a summer planting pumpkins. Now it looked like she was going to have to plant watermelons, too. She hoped she could get her miracle without having to raise a whole garden full of fruit and vegetables.

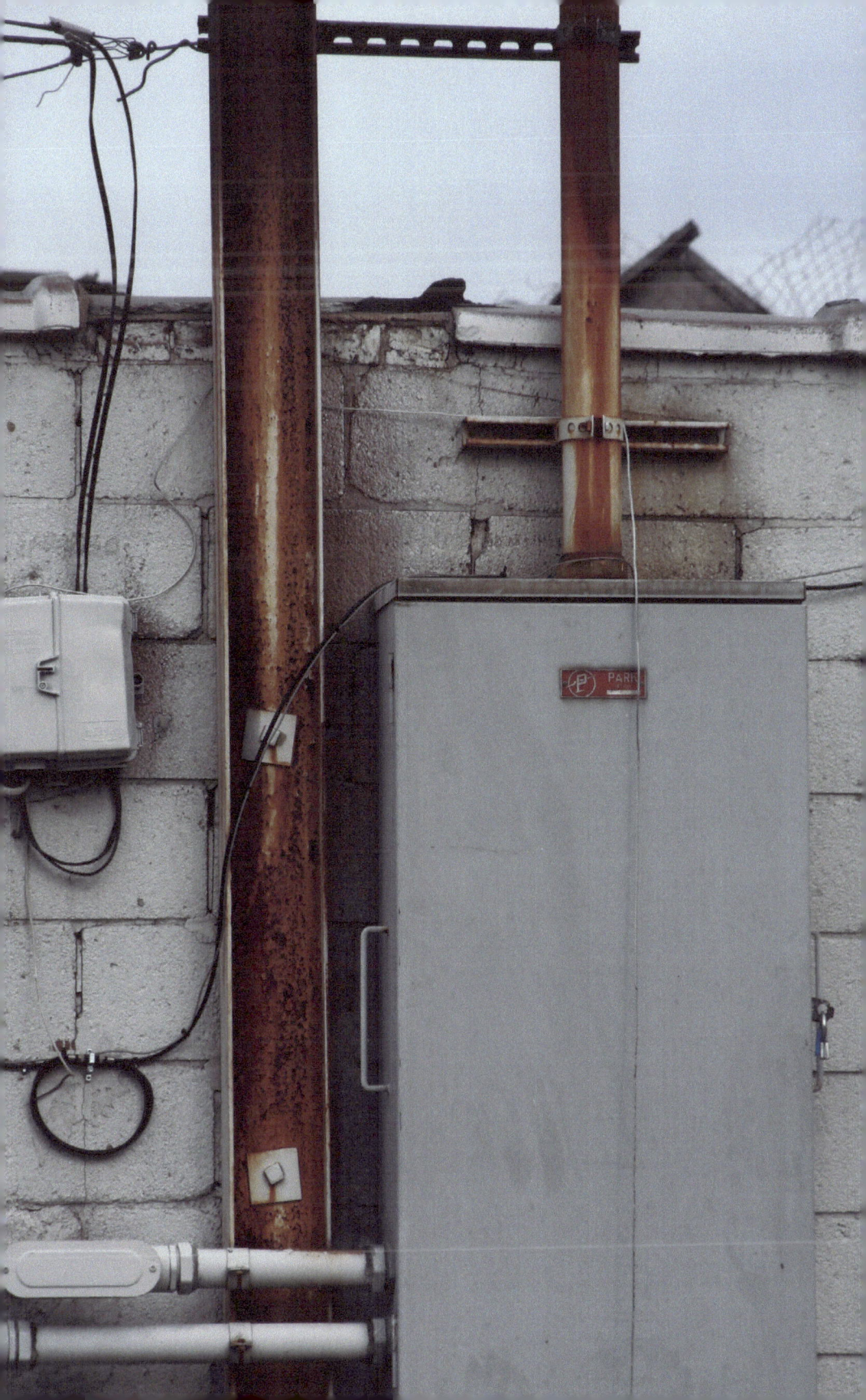

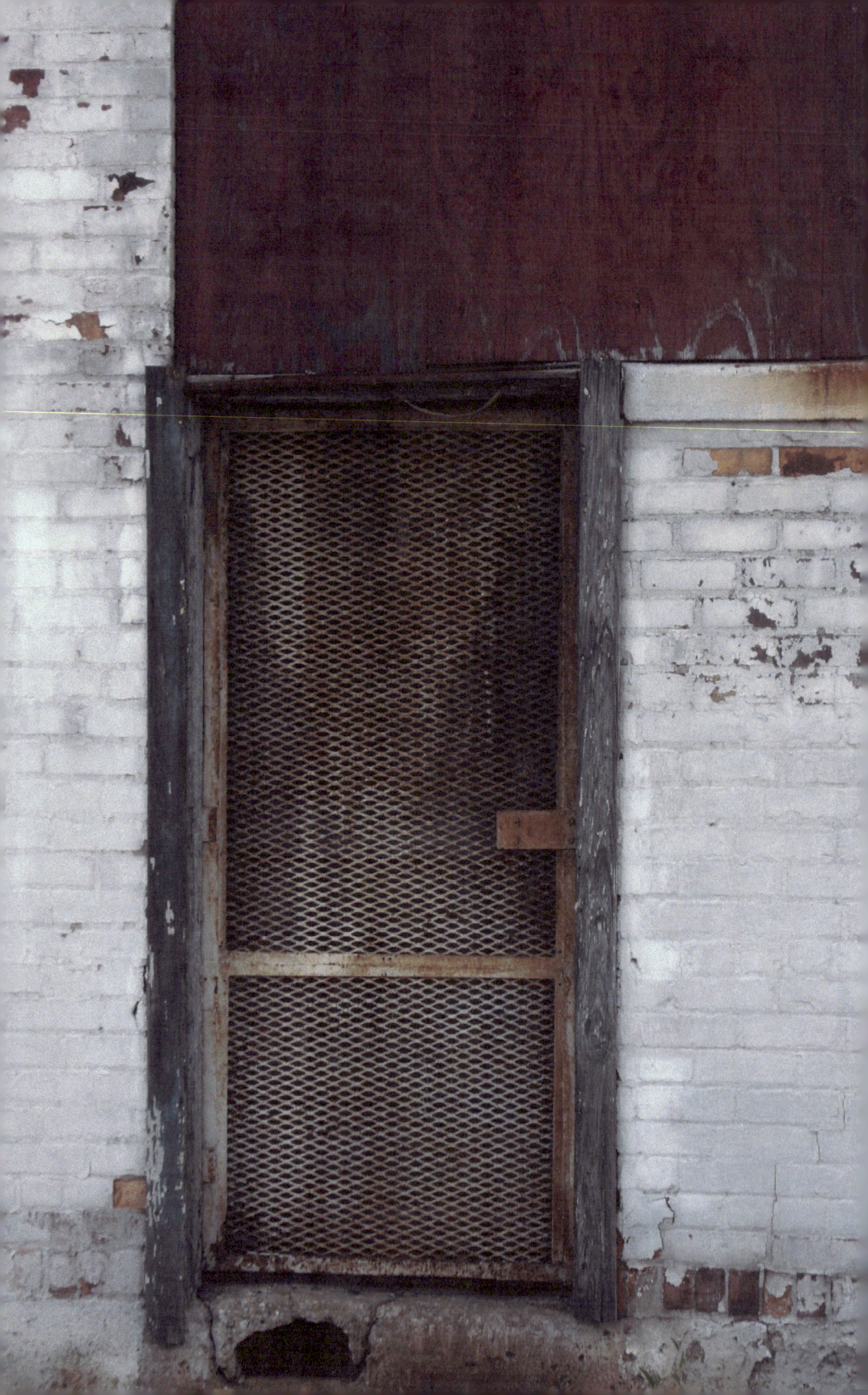

The bus appeared when Amanda reached the street. The door opened, and Amanda's grandmother waved. "Did you learn anything, dear?"

"I got a watermelon," she said. "And three seeds."

"Watermelon!" snorted her grandmother. "That old bird thinks they're good for everything. Anything else?"

Amanda hadn't intended to mention the pumpkins. She had wanted to get more practice with them, first. But she hadn't exactly hidden them either, so she showed them to her grandmother.

"Hmmm," she said. "Porcelain. I see. Well, you probably should do whatever you're good at. Maybe it'll come in handy. Let me look at those seeds." She didn't seem too impressed with the porcelain.

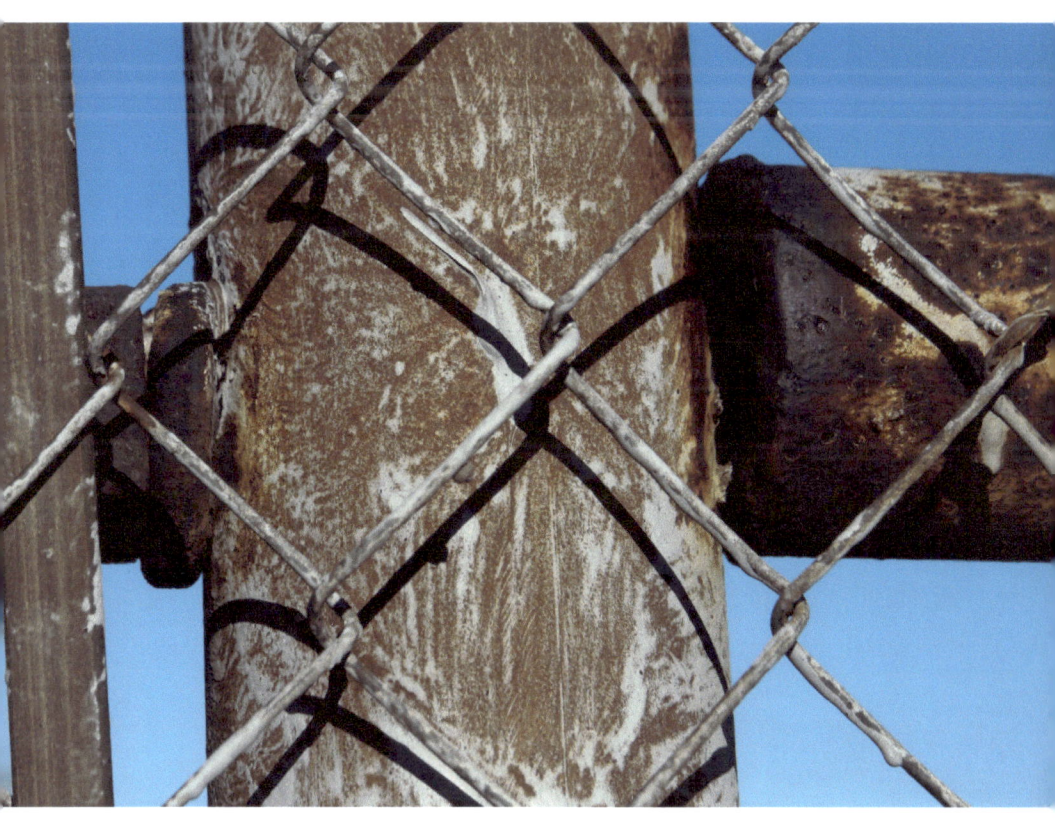

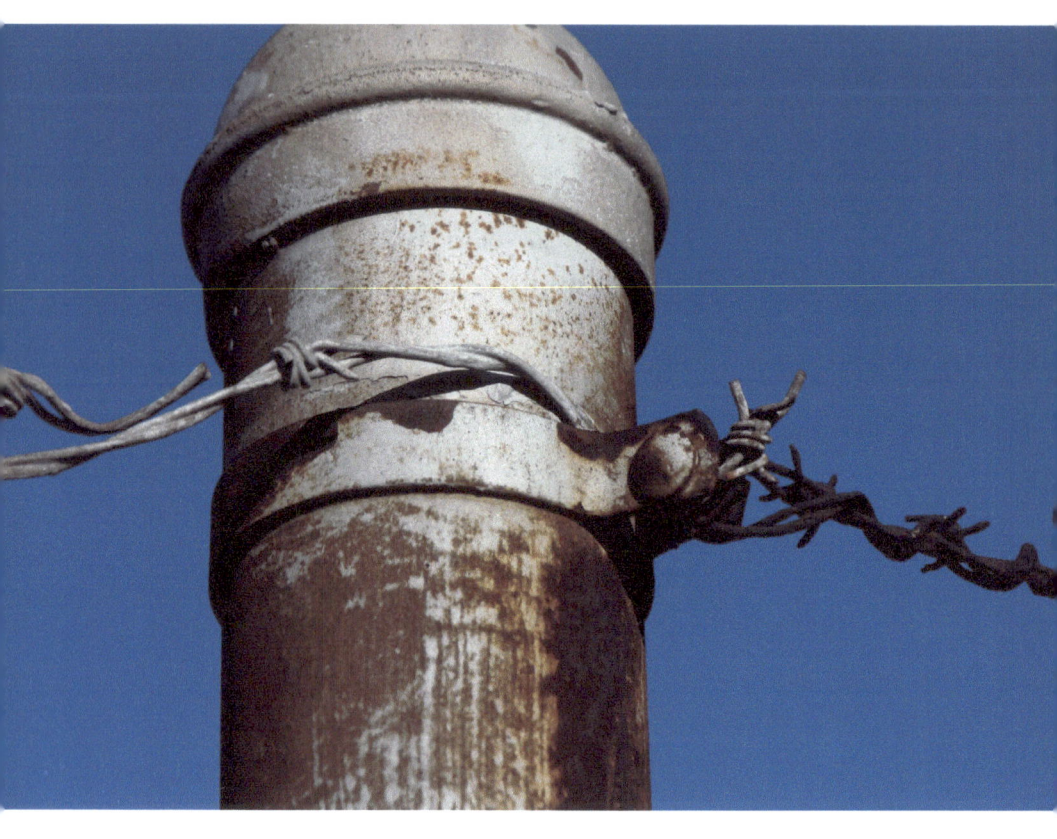

Amanda handed the seeds to her grandmother. Her grandmother's eyes widened. *Now* she looked impressed.

"These aren't watermelon seeds, Amanda. Maybe that old man *is* going to teach you something."

But she wouldn't say anything more.

~

Reflection questions

If you want to learn, you may have to talk to people you're not comfortable with. Who have you avoided that could teach you something you need to know?

Amanda's grandfather didn't think much of pumpkins. Amanda's grandmother didn't think much of watermelons (or, porcelain, though she was too polite to say much about it). *You* may have some gifts that other people don't value. What are you good at?

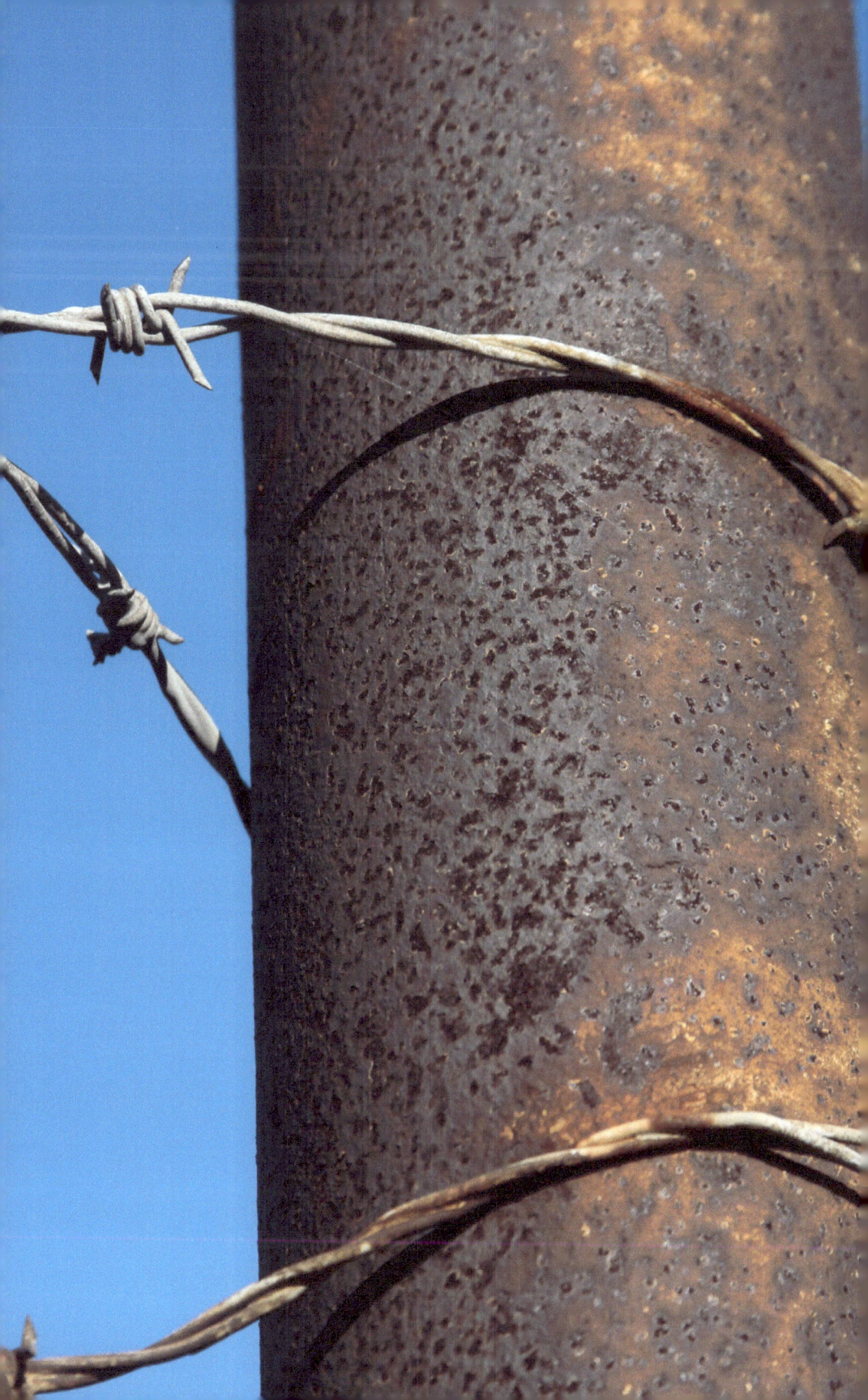

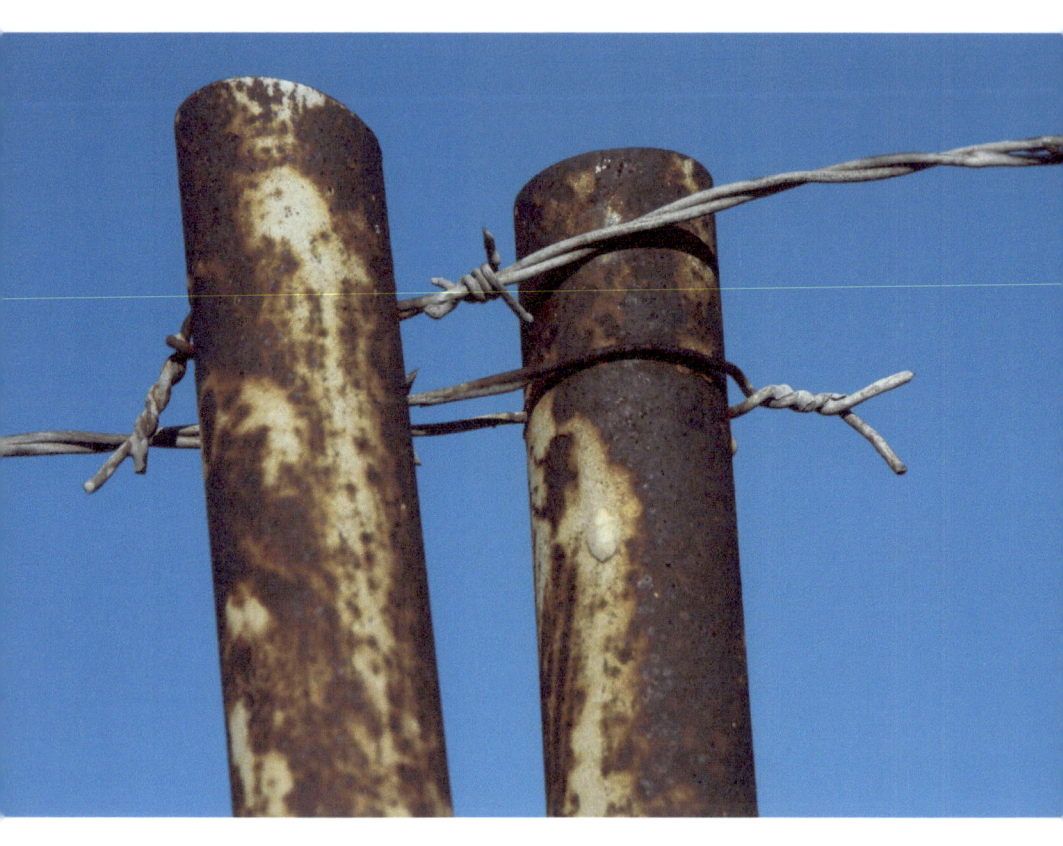

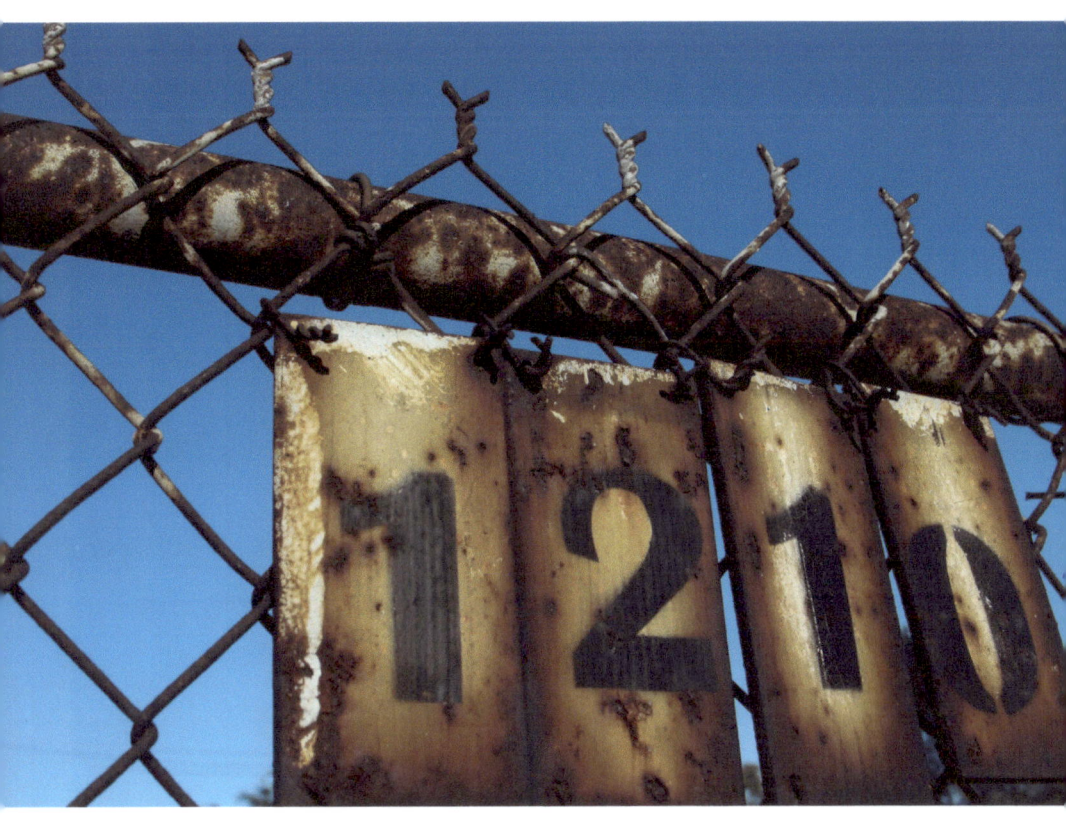

This Mark Dahle Portfolio includes a colorful painting, twenty-six beautiful photographs from Detroit, and a story about a carpenter who made fine furniture from scraps.

The carpenter came across the twig one day while scouring the countryside for debris. He had already found a sheet of plastic, a broken piece of plywood and several rusty, bent nails. Those he knew he could use. But the twig? He could not imagine a use for it. Nevertheless, it caught his attention as he walked along the edge of a forest. He absentmindedly picked it up.

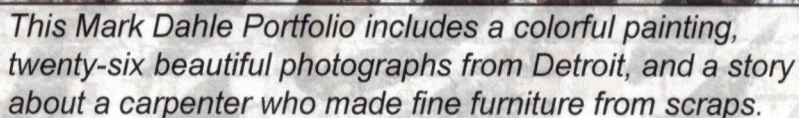

A Mark Dahle Portfolio

The
Carpenter
And
The Twig

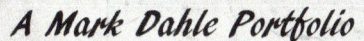

A Mark Dahle Portfolio

Amanda Gets A Surprise

(#3 in the series Amanda Wanted A Miracle)

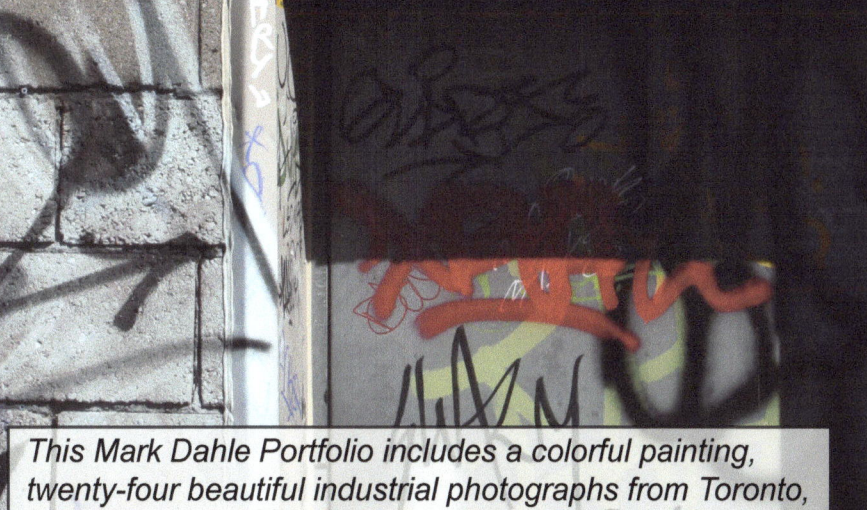

This Mark Dahle Portfolio includes a colorful painting, twenty-four beautiful industrial photographs from Toronto, and a story about a girl who wanted a miracle.

Amanda hated waiting. But eventually the snow melted and the ground thawed and – finally – it looked like it might be time to plant the seeds.

This Mark Dahle Portfolio includes a beautiful painting, twenty-five outstanding photographs from Manhattan, and the story of a busload of hungry passengers on a trip to the best restaurant in the world.

A couple hours into the journey, Jamil stood up and addressed the other passengers.

"Let's not wait," he said. "Let's stop on the way for a little bite – something just to tide us over."

CITY-GATES
QUEENS, N.Y.
718 939·9700

A Mark Dahle Portfolio

Mama Yah's Kitchen

www.ingramcontent.com/pod-product-compliance
Lightning Source LLC
Chambersburg PA
CBHW040917180526
45159CB00002BA/511